WHAT I HAVE LEARNED FROM LIVING

What I Have
LEARNED
FROM LIVING

TEN KEYS TO YOUR BEST LIFE

WRITTEN BY
JOANNE JOYNER

WHAT I HAVE LEARNED FROM LIVING

PALM TREE

An imprint of Palm Tree Publishing

Memphis, Tennessee

Copyright © 2019 Joanne Joyner

All rights reserved. No part of this book may be reproduced in any written, electronic, recording, or photocopying without written permission of the publisher or author. The exception would be in the case of brief quotations embodied in the critical articles or reviews and pages where permission is specifically granted by the publisher or author. Your support of the author's rights is appreciated.

WHAT I HAVE LEARNED FROM LIVING

Any parties seeking further information on this work should send inquiries to the author at:

jjoyner53199@gmail.com.

ISBN: 978-0-996077-5-6 (Digital)

ISBN: 978-0-9996077-4-9

(Print) ISBN: 978-0-996077-3-2b (Ezbook)

Original cover design by Les Solot

Manufactured in the USA

WHAT I HAVE LEARNED FROM LIVING

TABLE OF CONTENTS

THE FIRST KEY 13

Let Go Of Yesterday So You Can Embrace Today

THE SECOND KEY 22

Treat Every Person With Love And Kindness

THE THIRD KEY 31

Find Out What Your Gift Is

THE FOURTH KEY 38

Make Your World Better

THE FIFTH KEY 46

Continue To Evolve

WHAT I HAVE LEARNED FROM LIVING

THE SIXTH KEY 54

Eat Food That Is Good For Your Body

THE SEVENTH KEY 63

Be Slow To Anger And Quick To Forgive

THE EIGHTH KEY 72

Life Is One Choice After Another

THE NINTH KEY 80

Accept Responsibility For Your Life

THE TENTH KEY 86

Be Truly Grateful Every Day

WHAT I HAVE LEARNED FROM LIVING

INTRODUCTION

I am very happy and blessed my life has been a series of ups and downs, which have brought me to where I am today. My mother, Louise Palm, raised me with strong Christian roots. I grew up in the Church of Christ, and as a child, we would attend services every Wednesday and twice on Sunday. As an adult, I still harbor no ill feelings toward the Church of Christ and still have loved ones who take part. In my journey, I embrace my brothers and sisters from all corners of the earth and respect all Religious practices, even if I may not agree with their teachings.

WHAT I HAVE LEARNED FROM LIVING

If you know the philosophy of Church of Christ, you understand the strict doctrine that believes Church of Christ is the only true way of being saved from the fiery pits of Hell ruled by the devil. The devil being a horned demon cased away from Heaven. They believe you must be part of the church to be worthy of Heaven when Jesus Christ returns.

Even as a child, I had many questions and concerns about this strict religion that excluded folks like my grandmother, Martin Luther King Jr., and Gandhi from those considered "worthy", simply because they were not members. I questioned my pastor as a child, refusing to believe it could be true. My questions got me into trouble; the pastor told my

WHAT I HAVE LEARNED FROM LIVING

mother to keep me in check and said, "God said it, I believe it, and that is that." My mother pulled me aside and told me, "Child, stop bothering the pastor. This is the closest church to us and this is where we **are going**. She was telling me that she also was not taken with these teachings, but that the church is convenient and she had friends. The community was like a family and even though she did not believe the teachings, she loved the people. My mother did not drive, so we walked to church, it was convenient and the people were kind. I learned from Mama that you can be part of a church community without following blindly. She used to tell me, "The Bible also says study to show thyself approved!" In other words, study and get your own answers, so I did.

WHAT I HAVE LEARNED FROM LIVING

As I grew older, this church aligned less and less with my own evolving beliefs. When I had children of my own, I continued to take them to church because I wanted them to experience the culture. I would frequently look over at them during a service and whisper that what the pastor was saying was not completely true or accurate. If anything was said that was non-inclusive or hateful, I would discuss it with them on the way home.

Eventually, we left traditional churches and ended up practicing New Thought Ancient Wisdom. This philosophy of inclusion and love felt like home. The idea that I am an individualized expression of God resonates with my spirit and being a part of a non-

WHAT I HAVE LEARNED FROM LIVING

judgmental, loving place that allowed you to grow at your own pace was a welcome change. An environment that included every religion and non-religion was closer to my idea of what Godly spirit is.

I did what my Mama told me the Bible said to do; I studied to show myself approved. I studied everything I could get my hands on- every religion, ancient wisdom, and different spiritual practices from around the world. I took a little from each of them to arrive where I am today. My conclusion is that I am an individualized expression of God. I believe in one power, the power of the Creator. I do not believe in alternate powers; in my opinion, there is no horned devil holding a pitchfork that will come to get you if

WHAT I HAVE LEARNED FROM LIVING

you do not obey. I believe in the power of choice. I believe we are powerful god beings living a human experience.

Science has proven that humans have energy, and scientifically energy never dies. If that is true, the energy within us also never dies; you may call this a soul, spirit, life force, or whatever you wish. Regardless of its title, it continues on forever, even once we are finished using our bodies.

All that said, I believe we live a series of lives. I believe that in each life we are meant to grow and evolve, to learn all the lessons we are meant to learn and that our energy will return until we have finished

WHAT I HAVE LEARNED FROM LIVING

our task of evolving. This is what I have learned throughout my life. I do not ask anyone to believe as I do, that is for you to decide. You must learn your own lessons, and these are mine.

Throughout my journey, I have developed Ten Keys that have helped me to navigate through this life. I believe these Ten Keys will help anyone live their best life if they choose to practice them. I hope you will find that my book helps in some way.

Here are The Ten Keys to Living Your Best Life!

WHAT I HAVE LEARNED FROM LIVING

CHAPTER ONE- THE FIRST KEY

Let Go of Yesterday so You Can
Embrace Today

The first key is Let Go of Yesterday so you can embrace today. This chapter is about letting go of old habits. This chapter is about letting go of old beliefs. This chapter is about letting go of anger and resentment.

WHAT I HAVE LEARNED FROM LIVING

One of the things we all seem to have a problem with in life is letting go. Letting go is the beginning of change. Letting go seems very simplistic. Letting go should be something that we as humans should have very little problem with. Yet it is one of our greatest struggles.

Why? Why is it that we wish to hold on to our old stuff? Why is it that we wish to hold onto our anger and resentment? Why is it so much easier to hold onto those old beliefs, rather than embrace new ones? This is the million dollar question.

Have you ever gotten angry with a loved one? Have you ever gotten so angry with them that the anger you feel towards them almost feels like hate? Have you ever allowed this anger to become so deeply ingrained into your being that you found it all consuming?

This type of anger entangles you into such a web of resentment that you lose yourself. You start to feel out of character. You start to feel out of step. You become out of balance with the universe. You begin to search for that lost you. You begin to search for what you know is the truth of who you are. That is because you have lost the truth of who you are in the anger. You have lost the truth of who you are in the resentment. You have lost the truth of who you are in the hate. These states of being are not our true states

WHAT I HAVE LEARNED FROM LIVING

of being. We are not innately angry, resentful, or hateful. Our true nature is that of love and acceptance

That is why, when we live in a state of anger, resentment, and hate, we feel so out of sync with our true self. The reason why we feel so bad holding onto these three states of being is because it is completely out of character with our true state of being. It is as if we are trying to squeeze a square peg into a round hole. It just doesn't fit!

The definition of insanity is to do the same thing over and over again and expect a different result. Why do we continue to do the same thing over and over again and expect a different outcome? Why do we continue to hold onto our anger, resentment, and hate and expect to have the feeling that we desire? What is it that we desire so deeply in our souls? What are we crying out for when we continue to hold onto these things? I believe that we are crying out for love. I believe that we are holding on very tight to these states of being because we are hoping that our loved ones will change their behavior and show us the love we so desperately desire.

The problem is, it doesn't work. In all the years that I have been alive, I have never been able to use the recipe of anger, resentment, and hate to produce a product of love and acceptance. It simply does not work! If what you want from a loved one or simply

WHAT I HAVE LEARNED FROM LIVING

another being is love, then what you must give is love. To make a cake, you must use flour, sugar, and eggs. To get love, you must use love; that will get you the product that you want. You cannot use anger, resentment, and hate to produce a love response.

I have found that when I go to them with anger and resentment in my heart, then they normally respond in like manner. I have found that when I go to them with anger and resentment in my heart, then they normally respond in a like manner. They will normally respond, also, out of anger and resentment. That normally leads to a round and round and round battle that never ends. There is no resolution, nothing is fixed, and all parties concerned are sitting in a stew that continues

WHAT I HAVE LEARNED FROM LIVING

to boil. This is exactly what we do not want, yet we just don't know how to let go! We tell ourselves that we are not going to be the first to give in. We dig in for the long haul, waiting for the other person to do what we ourselves will not do. We wait for the other person to let go. If letting go is what we want from the other person, why is it so difficult for us to let go?

What are we waiting for? Why can't we just let go? I often wonder if we are waiting for a clap of thunder, or perhaps an earthquake! Are we waiting for a sign from God? Are we waiting for a sign that will tell us now is the time to let go? Are we waiting for something to jar us out of our stupor?

WHAT I HAVE LEARNED FROM LIVING

Well, stop waiting! There will be no clap of thunder! There will be no earthquake! There will be no sign above your head that says, "Now is the time to let go!" There will be no ceremony! So stop waiting, because there will be nothing but a simple change of mind from you. Yes, that is right, that's all there will be. There will be nothing but a simple change of mind; the same mind that you use to hold onto your anger, resentment, and hate will be the one you use to simply change your thinking. If you wish to snap your fingers and change your mind at the same time, you can do that. If you wish to close your eyes and change your mind at the same time, you can do that. If you wish to stomp your feet and change your mind at the same time, you can do that, too. The fact is that there needs

WHAT I HAVE LEARNED FROM LIVING

to be no special ceremonial condition. It's all you! It's always been all about you! You have two choices: you can remain in a state of anger, resentment, and hate or you can change, it really is that simple! You can choose to hate or you can choose to love. It's up to you! You decide right now if you wish to continue to hold onto yesterday or if you want to embrace today.

CHAPTER TWO- THE SECOND KEY

Treat Every Person with Love and Kindness

The Second Key is to treat every person with love and kindness. While this key should go without saying, it often needs a lot of explaining! Treat every person with love and kindness. Did I say every person? Yes, every person. Every single living being. Does this include people who are not so nice? Does it include people who choose to live their own lives full of hate? Does it include people who are not convenient or easy to be kind to? Of course! I know these people can often be the most difficult to love, but it may surprise you that they are often the ones who need it the most.

You may want to stop me right there and say "Ok you've lost me." Or "you've got to be kidding; there is no way I'm going to love a person who has done such horrible things." I get it; I know exactly where you are coming from. Some people are more difficult to practice this particular key on. That being said, in my experience, those who are the most difficult to love and care for are often the people who need it the most. I have also learned that the love you give to these people and every other person is the same love you will reflect back to yourself.

WHAT I HAVE LEARNED FROM LIVING

In essence, you are not only doing it for their benefit, but also for yourself.

Chances are, this is not the first time you have heard this rule; you may remember the Golden Rule: Do unto others as you would have them do unto you. It is a rule that many of us forget. We forget because there is so much anger and resentment in the world that it makes it so easy to forget to love and respect everyone we come across. This often happens when we need love and kindness the most.

When you approach each person you meet and greet with the spirit of love and kindness, it will make your own life much more fulfilled. Approach each person you encounter the same; ask yourself "where am I coming from with this person?" Ask yourself if you are approaching from a place of love, kindness, and compassion. I know it can be easy to assume some people deserve your ire, and perhaps that is true. I know you may feel some people are just not good enough for you to give the time of day. The fact is that no person is better than the next. A person may have made choices in their lives that may make them seem, in some instances, to be less of a good person in your eyes; conversely, you may reflect that way in another person's eyes. The point I am trying to make is this is all a matter of perception. Perception is what makes us all decide or make a judgement call on whom and what we think a person is all about.

WHAT I HAVE LEARNED FROM LIVING

A person's choices in life determine who they are, this is very true, but the same is true for you. If you come into contact with a person who has made the choice to hate a certain group of people, should you make the same choice and decide to hate them? Or should you be the bigger person and love them anyway? Sometimes, the very thing we hate is the mirror image of what we are taking on within ourselves.

The choice to treat each and every person with love and kindness is simply that, a choice. It is what you decide to do for you. As we discussed before, carrying anger, resentment, or hate in your heart is something that is counter to your very being.

WHAT I HAVE LEARNED FROM LIVING

So to come to anyone from a place of non- love is not only bad for them, but for you as well. In essence, you're not doing it for anyone else as much as you are for yourself. It feels so much better in your spirit and in your very soul to come from a place of kindness.

If you don't believe what I am saying, examine yourself the next time you come to a person out of hate. Stop for a moment and ask yourself if that hate brings you any joy; ask yourself if the hate brings you closer to God or the universe. If you are being truthful with yourself, you will likely find the hateful feelings bring discomfort rather than peace. On the opposite side of the scale, examine yourself when you go to a person out of love and kindness. You will find that you get more joy and peace from this. Showing love will resonate with your soul and also reflect back within yourself.

I think that you should ask yourself the question: what do I get out of being unkind to another person? If you examine that and look at it in an honest way, the truth will be that you likely do not feel good about yourself when you are being unkind. I think the hatefulness you are displaying is coming from a place of pain. Often, a person may behave in a cruel manner to another because they are also hurting on the inside. That person is often lashing out because they have either experienced a deep pain in the past, or the present which is causing them to project that feeling outward. We never know where a person has come from or what they are going through. All we truly know is where we have come from and what we are going through ourselves. At any time, we can decide if the place we are coming from is going to be a place of kindness. This is something we need to do for ourselves if we want to live our best life. It is not about the other person, but about you.

Love is a gift from me to you and from you to me, and it feels even better than a gift you might receive on your birthday! Love is a human's highest vibration; it is power and empowers every cell in your body. Love creates joy and happiness and it can even save the world. Do not add to the suffering of others

WHAT I HAVE LEARNED FROM LIVING

by spreading hate and pain. Do not add to your own suffering by allowing hate to fill you and then spew out into the world, causing harm to others.

Where is the good in any of that? Ultimately, it will be humankind showing love to one another that can save our world; we thrive on love and we are our best selves when we can give and receive love. Love your fellow beings and be kind to every person you encounter.

CHAPTER THREE- THE THIRD KEY

Find out what your Gift Is

The third key is to find out what your gift is; this is vitally important to your life. This key will take you on a lifelong journey. Indeed, some people spend their entire lives searching for this; others never begin, they may wander about their whole lives feeling they have a missing piece, yet never learn what it is. Everyone has been endowed with a gift that makes us who we are; it makes us unique. Your gift

WHAT I HAVE LEARNED FROM LIVING

distinguishes you from every other person.

Even though some people spend their lives looking for their gift, it is really not that hard to find. I believe the Creator has given us an easy road map to navigate through this existence. I believe that our gift is as natural as taking a breath. While we spend so much time trying to find our natural gift, we never stop to just breathe in the truth. The truth is that your unique expression of yourself will be **as** easy as breathing and if you stop for just a moment, it will reveal itself to you. It will show itself if allowed, because it comes from within you.

WHAT I HAVE LEARNED FROM LIVING

Your gift is the thing about you that comes to you so easily you wonder how it could be difficult for anyone else. Think for a moment: what is one thing you can do that people say "wow, that is amazing, how do you do that?" It is likely that the easy thing that you hardly notice because it comes so naturally is your gift. Many of us do not accept our gift for what it is, so we continue searching everywhere except within our hearts.

We are placed here on this earth to express ourselves in various ways as human beings. It is the individualized expressions that complete the world; the constant variety makes this planet work. Imagine if every person was the exact same! Imagine if there

WHAT I HAVE LEARNED FROM LIVING

was no difference at all between you and me! Imagine if we were all the same color, spoke the same language, looked and felt the same! A world without variety would be a world devoid of color. That would be a world without different voices and perspectives. Nobody would take chances because everyone would settle; in that world, no one would dream their own dreams. That would be a very boring world!

So I submit to you that the many shades of humanity are great. I submit to you that our differences are what make the world the beautiful place that it is. With this in mind, there is never a need to try to make others be the same as you. If everyone was just like you, it would lack the variety

WHAT I HAVE LEARNED FROM LIVING

and color. You and everyone else has a unique and wonderful gift to share with humanity.

Take a moment to think of that and let it sink in. Not only has the Creator given us life, it has given us a gift. Life in and of itself is a gift, and yet we are also endowed with this special, unique way of expression. Let that wash over you for a moment. Do you not feel an overwhelming sense of gratitude? I know I certainly do. I am in awe of life and in all the expressions life has to offer. It is very difficult to get bored with a life that has so many colors. If you are allowing yourself to become bored with this many faceted life you have been gifted, maybe you are not taking all that is offered to heart.

WHAT I HAVE LEARNED FROM LIVING

It amazes me that, not only do you have your special gift which is unique to you, but you also get to share the gifts that every other person has to offer you. You may say "I don't feel like anyone is sharing anything with me." Well, to that I say: when was the last time you listened to your favorite song? When was the last time you sat in your favorite chair? When was the last time you ate your favorite dish? When was the last time you drove your favorite car? When was the last time you saw your favorite movie? When was the last time you were in the presence of your favorite person? Every single time you experienced one of these things, you were sharing in the gifts of someone else's expression. The great thing is that doesn't even touch the surface of all the many gifts that you get to

WHAT I HAVE LEARNED FROM LIVING

share on a daily basis, let alone in your lifetime! Wow, how awesome is that!

Take the time to find out what your gift is. It doesn't matter if it seems big or small; the measurement of your gift is only what you make of it. You are special. You are unique. You have an expression that is uniquely yours. Take a breath. Take a moment. Take a lifetime if you choose, but find your gift.

CHAPTER FOUR- THE FOURTH KEY

Make Your World Better

The fourth key is to make your world better. I do men your world; while the world belongs to us all, the way to make it a better place is to each make our own immediate world a better place. What I mean is you and those around you. That's it. You do not need to worry about everyone in the world, or even everyone in the country, although if your reach is that vast, surely go for it. You do not need to feel responsible for your state, your parish, or your entire

WHAT I HAVE LEARNED FROM LIVING

city. Start right where you are, with you and yours.

So often people think when you say change the world that you are speaking of some grand scheme that will affect everyone on the planet! They often feel inadequate and not up to that big of a task. That way of thinking likely includes most of us, so don't feel guilty. It is a daunting task to try to change every person and solve every problem in the world. The good news is, that is not your task. You are only responsible for you and the world you interact with. If everybody worked toward that, the ripple effect would reach outward, and the whole world could indeed be better for it.

WHAT I HAVE LEARNED FROM LIVING

Let me let you in on a secret. Each one of these keys are intertwined and linked with one another. They work together in a beautiful symphony that create and works with life. Do you remember the Second Key? That was the key about showing love and kindness. And the Third Key, that was the one about finding your gift. It turns out those two keys will help greatly with the Fourth Key here, making the world better.

I hear you asking the question: How? I will tell you. Every person that you encounter and every person closely linked to you is someone you can affect in a small or even profound way. As I mentioned to you before, you never know where a person is coming from, or what they may be going through. Sometimes, changing the world could be as big as taking someone into your own home or as small as a few kind words.

When you discover what your gift is, you can use it to change the world around you. Let me give you an example. My oldest daughter has this wonderful gift that makes it easy for her to hear both sides of an issue and to diffuse conflict. She is able to be in the middle of two individuals having a heated argument and find common ground between them, then she can help them to a place where they can find a solution. It is a beautiful thing to watch. She does this so automatically and magically that it blows my mind. How many times have you seen individuals have a

WHAT I HAVE LEARNED FROM LIVING

disagreement then walk away and never speak to one another again? To have someone who can defuse it is beautiful! This can effectively save one relationship after another thus making the world a better place.

Another example is in me; I am a person that others feel comfortable coming to for advice. People seem to take comfort in the things I have to say. This has always been something that has come very easily to me. I take comfort in being there for my loved ones in their times of need. These gifts may not change the entire world instantaneously, but they can have a profound effect on one individual at a time.

WHAT I HAVE LEARNED FROM LIVING

Does making the world around you a better place mean you have to change someone's life in a profound manner? No it does not. I am not saying you need to go around searching for ways to make profound change. What I am saying is that when your situation presents itself, do what you can to make things better. This can be by very simple means; do not underestimate any kind gesture. Kind gestures may seem small to you, but may be huge to another person in a time of need.

For example, I once sent out a text to about 40 people. The text was basically reminding them of an event; at the same time, I reminded them that I loved them and that their presence was much needed and appreciated. I reminded each person that there was something special about them in particular being there. Although the text was sent to about 40 people, it was sent separately to each person. It was amazing to me when three people texted me back letting me know they really needed to hear that they were needed and loved on that particular day.

That brings me to the conclusion that making your world better does not have to be a major event. It doesn't have to be a life changing ordeal. As a matter of fact, it does not have to change you at all. The smallest thing can be a major thing in someone else's life. A small thing to you could be the kind word that makes another person's day. It could be the catalyst

WHAT I HAVE LEARNED FROM LIVING

for change in someone else's life. A small gesture can even save someone else's life. I have mentioned before that you never know what a person is going through; there are people who are but a moment from committing suicide. A moment that seems unimportant to you might save their life. There are people on the brink of losing everything and a moment from you might be that spark of hope.

You can make your world better one person at a time. You can impact the entire world one person at a time. Change can start today, with you.

CHAPTER FIVE- THE FIFTH KEY

Continue to Evolve

The fifth key is to continue to evolve. This key is very important; perhaps the most important task in our lives. I believe we come to this earth to evolve. I believe we are here to grow and learn life lessons. Learning life lessons is as important as figuring out what your gift is. Lessons we do not learn force us into repetitive life scenarios. In other words, we will face the same challenges over again until we learn the lesson. It is my belief that you can spend a lifetime or even multiple lifetimes- on the same lessons.

WHAT I HAVE LEARNED FROM LIVING

A few years ago, I wrote a novel called The Many Lives of Soulmates. This novel is about two gods named Zhan and Raya. The story is about Zhan and Raya coming from their planet of Edonia to Planet Earth to live a series of three lifetimes. These lifetimes will challenge them to find each other and evolve. They must evolve and become enlightened beings in order to return to their home. Like Zhan and Raya, I believe humans are on similar journeys throughout our lives. We must continue to evolve and enlighten during our lifetimes in order to learn and grow.

Indeed, if you are not growing then you become stagnant. If you are not learning you are standing still. If you do not evolve then why are you here? The

WHAT I HAVE LEARNED FROM LIVING

moment you stop evolving, you stop living your best life. You stop allowing life to flow through you. Many people become bored with life; at that moment, they cease the journey of exploration in life. A life that stops moving forward is a waste of precious moments. These moments cannot be relived. You can only live your best life in the here and now!

Everything is in a constant state of change. The very flow of life goes through different seasons. Even if you cling tightly to the past, everything continues to change around you, making it a futile battle. Even if you hold your mind hostage and do not allow it to evolve, your physical form will not obey the command. You cannot hold the same spot forever without losing your grip somewhere else. Look around you and at nature itself, it is in a constant flow of evolution. You are also a part of nature and, therefore, cannot expect to resist the flow of time. The best course of action is to go with it and evolve along the way.

It never ceases to amaze me that some people are faced with a life lesson that they continue to ignore. Even in the face of great pain, some people fail to notice they are doing the same thing over again in repetitive life scenarios. For example, some people choose abusive partners over and over. They go through terrible pain with a partner and when they finally get away, they do not grasp the lesson. They do not remember those characteristics or notice the red

WHAT I HAVE LEARNED FROM LIVING

flags in the next person who shows the same traits. Oftentimes, they choose another body with the same spirit as the last. If they had learned that life lesson they would recognize what they want and what they should avoid.

The best investment you can make is in yourself. We spend a lot of our lives investing our time into our jobs, our churches, and our relationships. We do not realize that if we spend more time developing ourselves, we will by extension excel in the other aspects of our lives. This is why it is so important to evolve and grow. If you continue to grow, learn, and evolve, you can make the world around you better, thus making the entire world better.

WHAT I HAVE LEARNED FROM LIVING

Spend some time reading self-help books. Spend time meditating. Spend time evaluating and writing out a plan for your life. Identify what you need to learn in life. I mentioned before that you should spend some time figuring out your unique gift; you should also spend time thinking about your life lessons. Think about your weaknesses; it is likely those are related to the lessons you need to learn. For instance, if you have a tendency to pick bad partners, perhaps your life lesson is to learn how to choose better. If you are the bad partner, your life lesson might be on how to be a better person. This is not always as difficult as you might think. I have found that deep down, we are aware, even if we may try to ignore them.

WHAT I HAVE LEARNED FROM LIVING

Life is much simpler than we often make it. We tend to make things more difficult by denying or ignoring the truth. We find it is easy to fool people and pretend. We find it easier to avoid being our true selves because we feel we are not good enough. What we fail to realize is that we have always been good enough. Though we may be able to fool many, or even all of the people, we can never fool ourselves and deep down we will know we are not being true. If you are searching your heart and feel uncomfortable with yourself, chances are you are on the wrong path. Learn to trust your inner spirit. Learn to trust yourself. Learn to look within and accept the truth.

WHAT I HAVE LEARNED FROM LIVING

Each day is a chance to be a better version of yourself. Each day is your chance to be a new and better you. It is your task in life to continue to grow and evolve. Make sure you are always moving forward rather than standing still.

WHAT I HAVE LEARNED FROM LIVING

CHAPTER SIX- THE SIXTH KEY

Eat Food that is Good for You

The sixth kay is to eat food that is good for you. This key can be a difficult one for many people because food is a necessity, we eat to survive. Food is also such a beautiful engagement of our senses that many of us often find it harder to resist overindulging. I must admit, this one is the hardest one for me. One of the reasons it is so hard is because it is so

WHAT I HAVE LEARNED FROM LIVING

confusing! The data on what you should eat is all over the map. Let's get into it.

For almost twenty years, I had been a strict vegan. For about five years, I added in some fish and chicken. About two years ago I became a fruitarian, which I did for about a year, almost exclusively. For the last year, I have eaten about 90% fruits and vegetables with occasional fish, eggs, and chicken; those may happen about once every two weeks. It all depends on my mood and my body. I have discovered that listening to my body's desire for nutrition is the best protocol for me.

WHAT I HAVE LEARNED FROM LIVING

Science seems to go back and forth on what is the ideal diet. I remember as a child eating eggs and that was good for you; then we were told no, that is bad. I remember eating butter, and then we were told that was bad. Now eggs are a super food and butter is better than most vegetable oils. Gluten is bad, so they say and now we have an abundance of gluten free products. I'm over all of it. I have decided just as we are all individualized spiritual beings we are also individualized physical beings. What works for one body may not work for another. Each one of us has to do the work to figure out what our bodies reject and what our bodies accept as good for us.

WHAT I HAVE LEARNED FROM LIVING

I have decided that a route of simplicity is better for me. I remember a time when we simply ate real food. My mother made food from scratch. When I was a little girl, I ate food like beans and cornbread. I had eggs and biscuits for breakfast. I had chicken, beans, and cabbage for dinner. I can remember my mother cutting up a whole chicken. I remember her soaking beans, and making cornbread from scratch. The difference between now and then is the chicken comes pre-cut and processed, whereas the chicken my mother made was a chicken that was alive, running around right up until it was killed to be eaten. The beans my mother made came straight from the ground; they were not from a can or pre-cooked and packaged. My mother's cornbread was made straight from cornmeal, never from a packaged box. That is the difference between then and now. So much of what we eat is pre-packaged and processed; a lot of it is not real food. If we could just go back to the simple days of eating real, fresh food, I believe we would be much better off.

I am not saying that anyone needs to be a strict vegan or a vegetarian or fruitarian. I am not saying that anyone should be paleo or any other prescribed diet. I am just saying that one should listen to their own body and through a process of elimination, as well as trial and error, find what works for you. Having said that, I do feel one should eat real food. I do believe

WHAT I HAVE LEARNED FROM LIVING

that one should eat whole foods; I do believe one should restrict their sugar intake and make as much as possible from scratch. For me, if I eat an overabundance of sugar, meat, and processed food, my body responds negatively. Therefore, I have wisely chosen to give my body the food that it functions most optimally with. For me, that means eating a majority of fruits and vegetables, with only occasional fish, eggs, or chicken. I have also found that my body does not function well with high alcohol intake, and so I limit that as well. I only drink on special occasions and, even still, only consume very little of it. It is unusual for me to drink more than a glass of wine. I say this to make the point that you need to listen to your body.

WHAT I HAVE LEARNED FROM LIVING

You must be in tune with yourself physically, spiritually, and mentally. I truly believe that we are divine beings, living a human experience. I believe that we are a threefold human entity; we have a physical, spiritual, and mental body. We are responsible for feeding and evolving all three of those bodies. Our responsibility living this experience is to be in tune with our divine consciousness. If you can master this, then you can also master your physical, spiritual, and emotional self. You cannot work on one aspect of yourself while neglecting the rest; all three must be a continuous work of love. I have spoken extensively about loving others and being kind to others. It is equally essential to love and be kind to yourself.

WHAT I HAVE LEARNED FROM LIVING

If you are not taking care of yourself, first and foremost, it is virtually impossible for you to care unconditionally for others. Self-love is indeed the greatest love of all. Self-love is where one must begin; once you master loving yourself unconditionally, it becomes so much easier to love everyone else. It is equally important for you to care for yourself mentally, spiritually, and physically. This is why giving your body the right foods that are healing and nourishing is so essential. If your physical body is not functioning at its highest level, it makes it harder to work on yourself spiritually and mentally. Everything about you is connected; you are a threefold being intertwined into one individualized expression. With this in mind, it is crucial that you feed your mind the right things, because what you put into your mind determines who you will become. It is important to feed your spirit the right things, because what you put into your spirit touches your soul. It is important to feed your body the right things, because what you put into your body touches every cell within you.

CHAPTER SEVEN- THE SEVENTH KEY

Be Slow to Anger and Quick to Forgive

The seventh key is to be slow to anger and quick to forgive. It may sound like I am being repetitive, but brace yourself because I'm saying it again: this is a very important lesson. Keep in mind- these are ten keys to help you have your best life. With that in mind, would each key not be profoundly important? Thus, my repetition of how important each key is. This one, however is very, very important.

How many times have you gone into an outright rage? Can you count them on one hand? Two hands? Or have there been so many times that you have lost count? How many times have you been so angry that you did not have control over yourself? Can you count that on one hand or two? Or is it possible that number is also too large to remember? If you find that these numbers are not easily counted, you are probably too quick to anger.

Do not misunderstand me, we all have moments when we become angry. We may also have those moments when we are simply enraged. Why? Well, sometimes it is because we have people in our lives that simply know how to push our buttons. Sometimes it is because our buttons are too easily pushed. Which one is it for you?

Perhaps you are in the category of those who have a certain someone in their life who knows how to push your buttons. If you are, then why? How often are you becoming angry with this button pusher? Is it happening once a year or once a week? The reason I am asking is because the frequency is important. As I mentioned to you before, all of us have our moments when we become angry and that is normal, it happens to us all. However, if you have a button pusher who

WHAT I HAVE LEARNED FROM LIVING

causes you to become enraged on a frequent basis, such as once a week or every day, you need to ask yourself why you keep that relationship. If you are not aware that it is outside the norm to be full of rage so frequently, then let me tell you: it is. If you wish to live your best life, it does not include frequent bouts of rage. Most of us wish to be happy more often than not; happiness and frequent or constant anger do not mix well, do they? So why do you choose to stick around a button pusher? Do you enjoy the chaos? I ask because some people do quite prefer chaos. Some people find chaos exciting and they stir up trouble to keep their lives and others in a constant state of chaos. If that is not you, then why are you surrounding yourself with people that bring out that side of you? You can decide

WHAT I HAVE LEARNED FROM LIVING

at any moment not to have this around you.

Seriously, you can decide to break the cycle of anger and chaos if you want to at any moment. You are the people you choose to be around. If you choose to be around people that bring out your anger and chaos, you need to stop questioning them and begin questioning yourself. Are they the problem, or is it really you? If you are choosing to remain in the situation, the problem may realistically be you. You do have a choice; maybe you are the button pusher and you are projecting yourself onto the other person. It is certainly possible that it is both you and the other person, but you can only be responsible for yourself. So let's start with you!

WHAT I HAVE LEARNED FROM LIVING

What are you waiting for to stop being an angry person? Do you expect thunder to clap and earthquakes to roll? Are you waiting on angels to sing or a sign from the universe itself? Let me let you in on a really big secret: none of that is coming! So now what are you waiting on? You can stop being angry and decide to forgive at any second you want! You can simply switch your mind from anger to release which leads to immediate forgiveness. Think about it. What normally happens when you decide to forgive? Is there a big fanfare, a parade? No, there is not; it is just you deciding to let it all go and forgive. That is it! And it comes to a full stop.

WHAT I HAVE LEARNED FROM LIVING

Think about the last time you forgave a friend or a loved one. What happened? Where were you? What was your mindset at the time? What were you thinking about? Sometimes, we hold out on forgiving someone because we want something in particular from the other person; some specification they must meet first. We have a few hoops they need to jump through. In other words, we are making it more difficult. We make it hard because we feel that person needs some kind of penance. Why is that? Often, we feel it is because that person has done us wrong and need some kind of punishment for whatever they did, so we hold out our forgiveness to punish them for what they have done. Now there are some really terrible people in the world that do horrible things, deserving of punishment.

WHAT I HAVE LEARNED FROM LIVING

I am focusing on your everyday person in our daily relationships. However, we still need to focus on forgiveness being for the offended, not the offender.s

You may ask: *What are you talking about, Joanne? That person broke my heart! That person cheated on me! That person stole from me! They said horrible things to me!* Yes, I know, they were awful! I'm still telling you to forgive them. Not only am I saying forgive them, but do it quickly.

Forgive them quickly so you can release the anger and resentment, as well as all negative energy from your spirit; do not let it fester and grow like a cancer. Forgive them so you can move on and be

WHAT I HAVE LEARNED FROM LIVING

happy; you are doing this for you, not them. Aren't you worth it? Be slow to anger and quick to forgive; there will be no fanfare or parade, but your best life is waiting for you to get back on track.

What are you waiting for?

CHAPTER EIGHT- THE EIGHTH KEY

Life is One Choice After Another

The eighth key is that life is one choice after another. Think about it. Life presents us with a plethora of choices! We are presented with so much to choose from, we do not always know where to begin. We over indulge on some choices and do not get enough of others. This key is where our free will shines. This key can be exciting and wonderful, because we are free to go in any direction with our lives that we so choose. It can also lead us to scary and dark places if we choose unwisely. Nevertheless, it takes us on a wild and winding journey called life!

Imagine yourself at a wonderful holiday buffet. There are tables upon tables of delectable treats. Tables piled high with meats, fruits, and vegetables from all over the world. Tables of cakes, pies, cookies and candies; the choices all so vast your heart dances. There are no restrictions on how much you can take. You are free to indulge in anything you want. Some people will get a large plate and go wild; they will take more than they could possibly eat. They will pile their plates high, they want it all. Other people will only take the things they know they can eat because they do not want to waste; they practice moderation. Still, others will take the smallest amount; they do not believe this feast could possibly be for them. They may look around to make sure it is really okay, but still take the smallest amount, depriving themselves.

Have you ever met a person who seems to have no limitations? They seem to freely go through life making all the choices that make them happy. They are the free thinkers who practice free will in abundance. These people seem to want to experience life to the fullest degree. They say yes to the extreme; they climb the mountains, jump from airplanes, and are willing to be the daredevils. They take the risks that many would not dare even consider. They believe the world is theirs for the taking. They start businesses that thrive, they accumulate large sums of money, and they are never satisfied with just a little but, they want it all and never stop trying to get it all. Do you know someone like this? You may say: *Wow, this person really sounds like they are living their best life.* Well, you might be right, but just because the person seems to have mastered their power of choice does not mean they have mastered all of the keys! Do not assume that their outer appearance is the total sum of their entire lives. You do not know them; you simply see how they appear when it comes to some of their choices in life. Their way is not wrong or right, it is just theirs.

WHAT I HAVE LEARNED FROM LIVING

Have you met this person? This person may try a lot of things, but does not feel compelled to overdo it. They do not see the need to jump from planes or climb mountains, but they may join the Peace Corps, fly in a plane, or go on a safari. They love experiencing life just like your daredevil, but they play it just a little safer. They may start a moderately successful business, be successful in their careers, and have great families, but they like to live on a smaller scale with less risk. While they may still do exciting things like traveling and trying new adventures, but stay more middle of the road in their adventures, rather than going off the beaten trail. They may avoid too much excitement in order to avoid bringing chaos into their lives. These people prefer more predictable outcomes;

they feel they deserve happy lives, so they plan and work for just that. Do you know someone like this chooser? Are you this chooser? This person practices moderation, and there is nothing wrong with that. It is not a right or wrong way, it is simply another choice.

The third person feels that they do not have many choices in life. They don't feel that they are as free to choose as the other two types of choosers. They feel that they are somehow blocked by other forces in their lives. Those other forces could be environmental, family, government, etc. These people do not feel in control of their own destiny. They often feel the shots are being called against them. They blame their conditions on other things. They may be unsatisfied

WHAT I HAVE LEARNED FROM LIVING

with their job or relationships, but feel it would improve if their own life was better. They feel like they do not have the power to change the things they are unhappy with. They dislike taking risks, feeling there is too much to lose and not enough to gain. They measure their success and happiness by the things they do not have. These people often feel deprived of the choices that they feel others have more access to; they feel unhappy, but at the same time unable to make any changes. Now, do you know this chooser? Might you be this one? Again, there are no right or wrong answers, just choices.

WHAT I HAVE LEARNED FROM LIVING

You could be one of the three people above, or you could be all three at different times of your life. The point is life is indeed a summary of all the choices we make. The choices you make determine the direction your life goes in. However, the good news is you can change directions at any time. That is up to you. Life is one choice after another; what is your next move?

CHAPTER NINE- THE NINTH KEY

Accept Responsibility for Your Life

The ninth key is to accept responsibility for your life. This key may be the hardest one to do out of all of the keys. Some people cannot and will not get past this key. That being said, you need to; it is paramount that you master the ninth key. It may be difficult, but you cannot glaze over it. You cannot work half-heartedly on this; you must do all the work in order to master this.

WHAT I HAVE LEARNED FROM LIVING

We just spoke about how the choices we make determine our life's direction. If that is true, then it is also true that you are responsible for those choices. I have seen people blame others for every little thing in their lives. I know a person who came to me angry with their best friend because she introduced her to a man who ended up cheating on her. She told me, "she should not have introduced me to a person like that."

I found it astounding how she could blame someone for another person's character flaw. How can it be your friend's fault that this person chose to do whatever he chose to do? Also, even if the friend introduced the two, it was her choice to engage in a

WHAT I HAVE LEARNED FROM LIVING

relationship with the other person. She was never forced to move forward after the moment of introduction. The hours upon hours after the introduction that were spent together were a choice. The consequences of the choices are your own to accept. You cannot blame another person for something that happens in your relationships, I told her. Even so, she continued down her path of blame and never repaired her friendship.

How often do we blame others for our problems? It is a daily occurrence. My friend once blamed me for getting lost because he asked me if I thought he should turn left or right and I chose right. The fact is, he made a series of left and right turns for

WHAT I HAVE LEARNED FROM LIVING

over thirty minutes. My one guess at a right turn did not change the fact that he was already lost. Also, he did not have to accept my guess; if you are driving a vehicle, you are responsible for where you end up.

If you are at a crossroad in your life and you must decide which way to go, remember that if you choose a road that takes you to a place of calamity that you were the one who decided to go there. I have seen people headed for trouble and even warned them of the trouble and they still decide to go right on into the trouble. The fact is you can't stop anyone from doing what they choose to do. When they choose to do whatever it is, you are not their scapegoat, and vice versa, they are not yours All adult humans must

WHAT I HAVE LEARNED FROM LIVING

face the fact that they are living their life choices.

That being said, we still have those who refuse to accept responsibility for their actions. They are determined to find a culprit, and to look outward for all their answers. They may do this because they feel it absolves them from the blame when the outcomes in their life are not to their liking. These kinds of people are always knocking on others' doors for help with their problems. Often, they don't trust their own judgement so they prefer to go elsewhere. The problem is, if it does not go well for them, they will blame everyone but themselves. You have to learn to say no to these kinds of people. It is best for them to learn to make their own choices.

WHAT I HAVE LEARNED FROM LIVING

If you find yourself unwilling to look in the mirror and know that you are the master of your own universe, then it is likely that you are the kind of person who blames others for your state in life. The truth is, you are the only one to blame for where you are in life. You have the power of choice to change your circumstances. If you choose not to, then you must accept where you are. Often, there is a lesson to be learned from every situation we find ourselves in. Try to learn something from your mistakes, and own that they are your mistakes.

The fact is that we are all the drivers in our lives. We determine which direction we will go every day, even if someone else gives us a hand now and again, we are still the one at the wheel.

CHAPTER TEN- THE TENTH KEY

Be Truly Grateful Every day

The tenth key is to be truly grateful every day. I cannot stress to you the importance of being truly grateful. This is one of the highest forms of vibration a human can have. If love is the highest, and I believe it is, this is the second highest. This key puts you in sync with the universe. To be grateful is to be warmly and deeply appreciative of kindness.

WHAT I HAVE LEARNED FROM LIVING

Being grateful, you might say: Oh, that's easy! I don't have to work very hard to be grateful. I would say that is true, it should not be hard to be grateful. However, some people confuse simply saying "thank you" with being truly grateful. It is easy to say "thank you"; it takes a little more thought and emotion to feel truly grateful. If someone makes you breakfast, you might say thank you rather quickly. I submit to you that is rather easy to do, but being deeply grateful that they thought enough of you to get up and take the time out of their busy morning to think of you when they really did not have to, places a bit more thought into gratitude. Thinking of the fact that they considered the food with love for you and perhaps even added something a little extra just because they knew it was your favorite. That goes a lot deeper than just a thank you.

When I say take time to be truly grateful, I mean just that. Take some of your precious time to be deeply and warmly considerate of the blessings you have; you are without a doubt blessed. You may ask how I know this, and I will tell you. You are reading this book right now, which means you are breathing. Have you considered your breaths? When you breathe, your diaphragm contracts and moves downward, this increases space into your chest cavity, into which your lungs expand. You probably never think about all the work your body puts in, just to produce one breath.

WHAT I HAVE LEARNED FROM LIVING

Nevertheless, it happens naturally. The Creator made it such an innate and mundane part of us that we hardly ever think about it. However, if we stop taking these breaths, within minutes we would die. Each breath is the gift of life. That is one thing we can all be truly grateful for. Secondly, if you are reading this book, you are probably of sound mind, or at least capable of reading. That is another thing to be grateful for; that means you are capable of choosing material that will help you better yourself. In my opinion, that means your mind is capable of processing thoughtful material. So you are truly blessed because you are breathing and thinking. These two blessings allow untold treasures to be at the tips of your fingertips.

WHAT I HAVE LEARNED FROM LIVING

I want it to be clear that I am speaking of being truly grateful for everything; do not overlook anything. Count your blessings, literally. I have developed a method that helps me count my own blessings daily. I start every day by being truly grateful. My method is called The Gratefulness Alphabet. With this method, I go through the entire alphabet and name something I am grateful for. Make sure you name things you are grateful for and attach an emotion to the thing. Think about it for a few seconds, rather than just picking something and moving on. Then move on to the next letter. I will list my method with some examples for you, so you can also begin being mindfully grateful.

WHAT I HAVE LEARNED FROM LIVING

The Gratefulness Alphabet

A - Air, automobile, ankles, atmosphere, acceptance, autumn, abilities, apples, accomplishments

B - Body, bath, bees, beauty, bounty, buildings, boxes, bananas, blueberries, bread

C - Care, community, completion, children, challenges, cake, calendars, cats, coconut, cherries

D - Days, dads, dancing, daughters, dirt, dogs, dandelions, daffodils, donuts, dollars

E - Everything, everyone, evenings, evolving, eternity, earth, eating, emotions, ears

F - Family, foundation, face, feet, fun, fabric, failure, facility, film, food

WHAT I HAVE LEARNED FROM LIVING

- **G** - Gratefulness, generosity, geography gentleness, genes, gardens, gains, goodness, grapes, granola
- **H** - Heart, hands, honey, happiness, habits, healing, hope, help, harvest, hugs
- **I** - Ideas, identity, imagination, impact, ice cream, ice, islands, inspiration, inclusion, inhaling
- **J** - Joy, jubilation, justice, jaw, jackets, jobs, joints jets, jam, juice
- **K** - Kindness, kids, keys, kisses, knees, kitchens, knives, kidneys, kinship, kale
- **L** - Love, light, living, land, language, lasting, laughter, liquids, lilies, luck
- **M** - Mothers, mankind, moon, motors, money, memories, magic, moments, mountains, melons

WHAT I HAVE LEARNED FROM LIVING

N - Niceness, nature, names, noses, necks, neighbors, needles, nation, nuts, newborn

O - Opportunity, optimism, openness, occupation, October, ocean, oranges, onions, occasions, opinions

P - Peace, people, palm, pants, parents, parks, paper, paint, peach, peanuts

Q - Quiet, quilts, quickness, qualifications, quality, queens, questions, quotes, quantity, quarters

R - Rain, remembering, rarity, raw, reach, range, railroad, radio, ripe, radish

S - Sunshine, sun, sons, seasons, stars, soap, savoring, soup, sound, satellite

T - Talking, taste, tomatoes, tongue, toes, tips, teeth, touch, time, teach

WHAT I HAVE LEARNED FROM LIVING

- **U -** Unity, Us, utility, umbrella, understanding, union, uniqueness, umpire, undergraduate, uncle
- **V -** Victory, visits, variety, voice, vegetables, vehicle, verbs, value, video, village
- **W -** Words, world, work, wonder, weeks, windows, walking, wallet, wind, wisdom
- **X -** Xenagogue (a guide), xenial (hospitable), xenium (gifts/presents), xenodocheum (hostel), xenophile (attracted to foreign styles), Xerox, xylophone, xo (executive office), x-ray, Xhosa (Bantu language)
- **Y -** Youth, years, yes, yesterday, you, yours, yellow, yawn, yard, yearly
- **Z -** Zeal, zest, zippers, zoo, zany, zealous, zazzy, zen, zippy, zingy

WHAT I HAVE LEARNED FROM LIVING THE WORK

Now that you know the Ten Keys, you must do the work. You must put them into action in your own life.

Start with the first key and practice it for twenty-one days, until it becomes habit. Each day, take note of what you are letting go of from yesterday when you first wake up. You can even do this while still lying in bed. Meditate. Focus on that for three minutes.

WHAT I HAVE LEARNED FROM LIVING

Then spend six minutes focusing on what you will embrace on this day. Keep your book next to your bed. Write both things down. Throughout your day, practice what you want, what you are embracing. If it is positive thinking, practice it. If it is being more efficient, practice it.

WHAT I HAVE LEARNED FROM LIVING

THE FIRST KEY- WORK PAGE

The first key is to let go of yesterday so that you can embrace today. The first key is so important that it requires twenty-one days of practice. At the end of each day, before going to bed, write down what you need to let go of for the day. Be descriptive so you can always go back and reference it if you need to. After letting go, write down what you will embrace. Here is an example: Day 1- I am letting go of my jealousy of my coworkers. I embrace that I am enough. I have every tool I need to be successful at my job.

WHAT I HAVE LEARNED FROM LIVING

Day 1

LET GO OF…

EMBRACE…

Day 2

LET GO OF…

EMBRACE…

Day 3

LET GO OF…

EMBRACE…

Day 4

LET GO OF…

EMBRACE…

WHAT I HAVE LEARNED FROM LIVING

Day 5

LET GO OF…

EMBRACE…

Day 6

LET GO OF…

EMBRACE…

Day 7

LET GO OF…

EMBRACE…

Day 8

LET GO OF…

EMBRACE…

WHAT I HAVE LEARNED FROM LIVING

Day 9

LET GO OF…

EMBRACE…

Day 10

LET GO OF…

EMBRACE…

Day 11

LET GO OF…

EMBRACE…

Day 12

LET GO OF…

EMBRACE…

WHAT I HAVE LEARNED FROM LIVING

Day 13

LET GO OF...

EMBRACE...

Day 14

LET GO OF...

EMBRACE...

Day 15

LET GO OF...

EMBRACE...

Day 16

LET GO OF...

EMBRACE...

WHAT I HAVE LEARNED FROM LIVING

Day 17

LET GO OF…

EMBRACE…

Day 18

LET GO OF…

EMBRACE…

Day 19

LET GO OF…

EMBRACE…

Day 20

LET GO OF…

EMBRACE…

WHAT I HAVE LEARNED FROM LIVING

Day 21

LET GO OF…

EMBRACE…

THE SECOND KEY- WORK PAGE

The second key must be practiced exclusively for ten days. Please actively practice treating people with kindness and love. At the end of each day, write down who you were able to touch and affect with your conscious effort. Detail your events. Do this for ten days before moving on to the next key.

WHAT I HAVE LEARNED FROM LIVING

Day 1

Who did I treat with love and kindness today? How?

Day 2

Who did I treat with love and kindness today? How?

Day 3

Who did I treat with love and kindness today? How?

Day 4

Who did I treat with love and kindness today? How?

Day 5

Who did I treat with love and kindness today? How?

WHAT I HAVE LEARNED FROM LIVING

Day 6

Who did I treat with love and kindness today? How?

Day 7

Who did I treat with love and kindness today? How?

Day 8

Who did I treat with love and kindness today? How?

Day 9

Who did I treat with love and kindness today? How?

Day 10

Who did I treat with love and kindness today? How?

WHAT I HAVE LEARNED FROM LIVING

THE THIRD KEY- WORK PAGE

The third key is to find out what your gift is. This key should be worked on exclusively for ten days. This key will come to you as you spend these ten days focusing on what you love to do. Focus on what comes to you easily. This key is completely your job to find out, It is very possible that you may have more than one gift. Often these gifts are connected in some way. For ten days, ask yourself what you love doing and what you did to practice your gift.

WHAT I HAVE LEARNED FROM LIVING

Day 1

What do you love doing? How did you practice today?

Day 2

What do you love doing? How did you practice today?

Day 3

What do you love doing? How did you practice today?

Day 4

What do you love doing? How did you practice today?

Day 5

What do you love doing? How did you practice today?

WHAT I HAVE LEARNED FROM LIVING

Day 6

What do you love doing? How did you practice today?

Day 7

What do you love doing? How did you practice today?

Day 8

What do you love doing? How did you practice today?

Day 9

What do you love doing? How did you practice today?

Day 10

What do you love doing? How did you practice today?

THE FOURTH KEY- WORK PAGE

The Fourth Key is to make your world better. This key requires ten days of singular practice. As I explained in chapter four, you will be making your world better You will be focusing on your immediate world. Just focus on where you have the ability to affect.

It is best to focus on something or someone that you can help. This could be as simple as a kind word or as big as giving someone a car.

WHAT I HAVE LEARNED FROM LIVING

You decide based on your ability and capacity and the needs and concerns of the people you encounter every day. For ten days, make this your focus. Record your event(s) daily. Be descriptive, so that when you go back to review your effort it will inspire you to keep doing it!

Day 1

How did you make your world better?

Day 2

How did you make your world better?

WHAT I HAVE LEARNED FROM LIVING

Day 3

How did you make your world better?

Day 4

How did you make your world better?

Day 5

How did you make your world better?

Day 6

How did you make your world better?

WHAT I HAVE LEARNED FROM LIVING

Day 7

How did you make your world better?

Day 8

How did you make your world better?

Day 9

How did you make your world better?

Day 10

How did you make your world better?

THE FIFTH KEY- WORK PAGE

The fifth key is to continue to evolve. This key will require some study and possible research. I have found meditation to be quite helpful. The goal here is to grow and to expand your mind and awareness of who you are.

You will need to spend twenty-one days working with just this key. It is very important to make this key a habit. It should become your life's journey to evolve and learn. Each day of the twenty-one days,

WHAT I HAVE LEARNED FROM LIVING

You should study material or people that help you to grow. Write down key influences and influencers that stick with you. Write down events and occurrences that are life-altering or edifying. Write down what you learn each day.

Day 1

What did you learn today?

Day 2

What did you learn today?

Day 3

What did you learn today?

WHAT I HAVE LEARNED FROM LIVING

Day 4

What did you learn today?

Day 5

What did you learn today?

Day 6

What did you learn today?

Day 7

What did you learn today?

WHAT I HAVE LEARNED FROM LIVING

Day 8

What did you learn today?

Day 9

What did you learn today?

Day 10

What did you learn today?

Day 11

What did you learn today?

WHAT I HAVE LEARNED FROM LIVING

Day 12

What did you learn today?

Day 13

What did you learn today?

Day 14

What did you learn today?

Day 15

What did you learn today?

WHAT I HAVE LEARNED FROM LIVING

Day 16

What did you learn today?

Day 17

What did you learn today?

Day 18

What did you learn today?

Day 19

What did you learn today?

WHAT I HAVE LEARNED FROM LIVING

Day 20

What did you learn today?

Day 21

What did you learn today?

WHAT I HAVE LEARNED FROM LIVING

THE SIXTH KEY- WORK PAGE

The Sixth Key is to eat food that is good for your body. This key again should be your singular key focus for twenty-one days. It is my hope that you will continue this key even after the program.

Remember to eat 70% fruits and vegetables and about 30% ocean fish and free range chicken. Stick with whole foods and grains. Stay away from processed and pre-packaged food. Keep it simple; eat like your grandparents ate. Eat food that is good for your body. Write down your meals each day and how you feel after

WHAT I HAVE LEARNED FROM LIVING

Day 1

What did you eat today and how did you feel after?

Breakfast-

Lunch-

Dinner-

Snacks-

Day 2

What did you eat today and how did you feel after?

Breakfast-

Lunch-

Dinner-

Snacks-

WHAT I HAVE LEARNED FROM LIVING

Day 3

What did you eat today and how did you feel after?

Breakfast-

Lunch-

Dinner-

Snacks-

Day 4

What did you eat today and how did you feel after?

Breakfast-

Lunch-

Dinner-

Snacks-

WHAT I HAVE LEARNED FROM LIVING

Day 5

What did you eat today and how did you feel after?

Breakfast-

Lunch-

Dinner-

Snacks-

Day 6

What did you eat today and how did you feel after?

Breakfast-

Lunch-

Dinner-

Snacks-

WHAT I HAVE LEARNED FROM LIVING

Day 7

What did you eat today and how did you feel after?

Breakfast-

Lunch-

Dinner-

Snacks-

Day 8

What did you eat today and how did you feel after?

Breakfast-

Lunch-

Dinner-

Snacks-

WHAT I HAVE LEARNED FROM LIVING

Day 9

What did you eat today and how did you feel after?

Breakfast-

Lunch-

Dinner-

Snacks-

Day 10

What did you eat today and how did you feel after?

Breakfast-

Lunch-

Dinner-

Snacks-

WHAT I HAVE LEARNED FROM LIVING

Day 11

What did you eat today and how did you feel after?

Breakfast-

Lunch-

Dinner-

Snacks-

Day 12

What did you eat today and how did you feel after?

Breakfast-

Lunch-

Dinner-

Snacks-

WHAT I HAVE LEARNED FROM LIVING

Day 13

What did you eat today and how did you feel after?

Breakfast-

Lunch-

Dinner-

Snacks-

Day 14

What did you eat today and how did you feel after?

Breakfast-

Lunch-

Dinner-

Snacks-

WHAT I HAVE LEARNED FROM LIVING

Day 15

What did you eat today and how did you feel after?

Breakfast-

Lunch-

Dinner-

Snacks-

Day 16

What did you eat today and how did you feel after?

Breakfast-

Lunch-

Dinner-

Snacks-

WHAT I HAVE LEARNED FROM LIVING

Day 17

What did you eat today and how did you feel after?

Breakfast-

Lunch-

Dinner-

Snacks-

Day 18

What did you eat today and how did you feel after?

Breakfast-

Lunch-

Dinner-

Snacks-

WHAT I HAVE LEARNED FROM LIVING

Day 19

What did you eat today and how did you feel after?

Breakfast-

Lunch-

Dinner-

Snacks-

Day 20

What did you eat today and how did you feel after?

Breakfast-

Lunch-

Dinner-

Snacks-

WHAT I HAVE LEARNED FROM LIVING

Day 21

What did you eat today and how did you feel after?

Breakfast-

Lunch-

Dinner-

Snacks-

WHAT I HAVE LEARNED FROM LIVING

THE SEVENTH KEY- WORK PAGE

The Seventh key is to be slow to anger and quick to forgive. This key will require fourteen days of singular practice. You will really need to focus on being slow to anger. Practice expecting people to say what they feel and being ok with them saying it. Practice knowing that their truth may not be the same as your own. Remain in a perpetual state of love and forgiveness. If you do get angry, forgive quickly and forgive for yourself. If others wish to remain in a rut of anger, do not take up residence with them, move on.

WHAT I HAVE LEARNED FROM LIVING

Write down what you were bothered by each day. Write down after that: I release it. I forgive me. I forgive them. All is well.

Here is an example: Day 1… I am angry about her yelling at me. I release it. I forgive me. I forgive her. All is well.

Day 1
Who did you forgive today?

Day 2
Who did you forgive today?

WHAT I HAVE LEARNED FROM LIVING

Day 3

Who did you forgive today?

Day 4

Who did you forgive today?

Day 5

Who did you forgive today?

Day 6

Who did you forgive today?

Day 7

Who did you forgive today?

WHAT I HAVE LEARNED FROM LIVING

Day 8

Who did you forgive today?

Day 9

Who did you forgive today?

Day 10

Who did you forgive today?

Day 11

Who did you forgive today?

Day 12

Who did you forgive today?

WHAT I HAVE LEARNED FROM LIVING

Day 13

Who did you forgive today?

Day 14

Who did you forgive today?

THE EIGHTH KEY-WORK PAGE

The eighth key is life is one choice after another. This key makes you who you are. You should be more thoughtful about the choices you make.

This key should be practiced for seven days singularly. Each day, you should track the most important life choice you made for the day, write it down and write how it will affect your life. Ask yourself if it was a good choice; if it is not, change it.

WHAT I HAVE LEARNED FROM LIVING

Here is an example: Day 1… I have decided to leave my job. My job causes a lot of stress and makes me unhappy. I think this is a good choice, because I have discovered my gift. I will start a new career.

Day 1

What life choices did you make today?

Day 2

What life choices did you make today?

Day 3

What life choices did you make today?

WHAT I HAVE LEARNED FROM LIVING

Day 4

What life choices did you make today?

Day 5

What life choices did you make today?

Day 6

What life choices did you make today?

Day 7

What

THE NINTH KEY- WORK PAGE

The Ninth Key is to accept responsibility for your life. This key needs to be a habit and requires twenty-one days of singular practice. This may be one of the most difficult keys to master.

You will need to write down each day what you take responsibility for in your life and what you will do to change, if needed.

Here is an example: Day 1… I accept responsibility for breaking my promise. I will apologize and fulfil my promises in the future.

WHAT I HAVE LEARNED FROM LIVING

Day 1

I accept responsibility for...

Day 2

I accept responsibility for...

Day 3

I accept responsibility for...

Day 4

I accept responsibility for...

Day 5

I accept responsibility for...

WHAT I HAVE LEARNED FROM LIVING

Day 6

I accept responsibility for...

Day 7

I accept responsibility for...

Day 8

I accept responsibility for...

Day 9

I accept responsibility for...

Day 10

I accept responsibility for...

WHAT I HAVE LEARNED FROM LIVING

Day 11

I accept responsibility for...

Day 12

I accept responsibility for...

Day 13

I accept responsibility for...

Day 13

I accept responsibility for...

Day 15

I accept responsibility for...

WHAT I HAVE LEARNED FROM LIVING

Day 16

I accept responsibility for...

Day 17

I accept responsibility for...

Day 18

I accept responsibility for...

Day 19

I accept responsibility for...

Day 20

I accept responsibility for...

Day 21

I accept responsibility for...

WHAT I HAVE LEARNED FROM LIVING

THE TENTH KEY- WORK PAGE

The Tenth Key is to be truly grateful every day. This key is a high vibration key and feels wonderful to practice. This key requires fourteen days of singular practice.

Remember to spend time truly feeling grateful. Each of the next fourteen days you will do the Gratefulness Alphabet. Just say one thing per letter. Start when you first get up or even while still in bed. It does not take as long as you might think. Recite what you are grateful for in the morning, Say it out loud, and bask in it. At night, take the time to write it down.

Day 1

What are you truly grateful for?

Day 2

What are you truly grateful for?

Day 3

What are you truly grateful for?

Day 4

What are you truly grateful for?

WHAT I HAVE LEARNED FROM LIVING

Day 5

What are you truly grateful for?

Day 6

What are you truly grateful for?

Day 7

What are you truly grateful for?

Day 8

What are you truly grateful for?

Day 9

What are you truly grateful for?

WHAT I HAVE LEARNED FROM LIVING

Day 10

What are you truly grateful for?

Day 12

What are you truly grateful for?

Day 13

What are you truly grateful for?

Day 14

What are you truly grateful for?

WHAT I HAVE LEARNED FROM LIVING

SUMMARY

By now, you have completed your work. If done properly it took 149 days of work. How do you feel? For ten days, say all ten keys out loud each day. Incorporate them into your daily life. Live them. When you master them, I hope you will find yourself living your best life.

Here is the full list of the keys. Read them aloud every day for ten days.

First Key- Let go of yesterday and embrace today.

WHAT I HAVE LEARNED FROM LIVING

Second Key- Treat every person with love and kindness.

Third Key- Find out what your gift is.

Fourth Key- Make your world better.

Fifth Key-Continue to evolve.

Sixth Key- Eat food that is good for your body.

Seventh Key- Be slow to anger and quick to forgive.

Eighth Key- Life is one choice after another.

WHAT I HAVE LEARNED FROM LIVING

Ninth Key- Accept responsibility in your life.

Tenth Key- Be truly grateful every day.

And so it is…

ABOUT THE AUTHOR

Joanne Joyner is an author, life coach, singer, songwriter, a mom and a wife. She is on a life journey of constant spiritual evolution and self- growth. She has five beautiful children. She lives in Tennessee with her loving husband Philip.

ACKNOWLEDGEMENTS

I would like to thank my husband, Philip who is my soulmate. I thank my children, Jessica, Jas, Jalisa, Andrew, and Jonathon, who are my constant inspiration. I thank my mother, Louise Palm, who taught me the meaning of unconditional love. I thank my spiritual leader, John Gilmore, who coined the term "individualized expressions of God." He helped me to walk down the path of spiritual awakening.

www.ingramcontent.com/pod-product-compliance
Lightning Source LLC
Chambersburg PA
CBHW070156100426
42743CB00013B/2938